Štěpán Braňka

On 1984 & A Clockwork Orange

Sunderland College

Bede/Headways Learning Centre

This book is due for return on or before the last date shown below
Please be aware that sanctions are applied for overdue items
Renew online via Moodle
Renew by phone: call 5116344

- 7 OCT 2022		
- 9 NOV 2022		

Author _Branka, S._

Class _820 · 093_   Location Code _ELI_

21 DAY LOAN

Štěpán Braňka

On 1984 & A Clockwork Orange

Analysis and comparison of dystopian motifs in Anthony Burgess' and George Orwell's novels

LAP LAMBERT Academic Publishing

Impressum / Imprint
Bibliografische Information der Deutschen Nationalbibliothek: Die Deutsche Nationalbibliothek verzeichnet diese Publikation in der Deutschen Nationalbibliografie; detaillierte bibliografische Daten sind im Internet über http://dnb.d-nb.de abrufbar.
Alle in diesem Buch genannten Marken und Produktnamen unterliegen warenzeichen-, marken- oder patentrechtlichem Schutz bzw. sind Warenzeichen oder eingetragene Warenzeichen der jeweiligen Inhaber. Die Wiedergabe von Marken, Produktnamen, Gebrauchsnamen, Handelsnamen, Warenbezeichnungen u.s.w. in diesem Werk berechtigt auch ohne besondere Kennzeichnung nicht zu der Annahme, dass solche Namen im Sinne der Warenzeichen- und Markenschutzgesetzgebung als frei zu betrachten wären und daher von jedermann benutzt werden dürften.

Bibliographic information published by the Deutsche Nationalbibliothek: The Deutsche Nationalbibliothek lists this publication in the Deutsche Nationalbibliografie; detailed bibliographic data are available in the Internet at http://dnb.d-nb.de.
Any brand names and product names mentioned in this book are subject to trademark, brand or patent protection and are trademarks or registered trademarks of their respective holders. The use of brand names, product names, common names, trade names, product descriptions etc. even without a particular marking in this works is in no way to be construed to mean that such names may be regarded as unrestricted in respect of trademark and brand protection legislation and could thus be used by anyone.

Coverbild / Cover image: www.ingimage.com

Verlag / Publisher:
LAP LAMBERT Academic Publishing
ist ein Imprint der / is a trademark of
AV Akademikerverlag GmbH & Co. KG
Heinrich-Böcking-Str. 6-8, 66121 Saarbrücken, Deutschland / Germany
Email: info@lap-publishing.com

Herstellung: siehe letzte Seite /
Printed at: see last page
ISBN: 978-3-659-40969-1

Acknowledgement

I would like to express my gratitude to my supervisor PhDr. Petr Chalupský, Ph.D. and I would like to thank him for his dedicated help and support throughout the writing of this work.

Content:

I. Introduction 2

II. Theoretical part: Background and Inspirations 4

   II.1. Influence and Historical Importance 4

   II.2. A Prophecy not Too Far in the Future... 6

   II.3. Personal Background... 7

      II.3.1 George Orwell.. 7

      II.3.2 Anthony Burgess 8

   II.4. Symbolism:... 10

   II.5. Origins of Totalitarian Themes.. 12

      II.5.1 Methods and Reasons 12

      II.5.2 The Language 15

III. Practical Part – Two Worlds 17

   III.1. Atmosphere of the Cities.. 17

   III.2. The Society 19

   III.3. Totalitarian Methods... 21

      III.3.1 Methods of the Party 21

      III.3.2 People Turned into Clockwork Oranges 24

   III.4. Dystopias Side by Side... 26

   III.5. Winston Smith and Alex and their Development throughout the Novel.. 27

      III.5.1 Hero vs. Antihero... 27

      III.5.2 The Beginning of the End. 29

      III.5.3 Betrayal and How Protagonists are Being Used. 30

   III.6. Newspeak and Nadsat 33

      III.6.1 Brief Analyssis.. 33

      III.6.2 Other Language Finesses in *A Clockwork Orange* 35

      III.6.3 Purposes and Effects 36

IV. Conclusion 38

I. Introduction

The police, interrogations, propaganda, murder, political manipulations and oppression, loss of individual freedom are the leitmotifs of most dystopian novels. Both *1984* and *A Clockwork Orange* that this work focuses on by no means violate this rule. The aim of this work is to analyze and to compare how both authors present their dystopias in these two novels, characterize their protagonists and their position in the corrupted world they inhabit. However, heroes (or antiheroes) of these novels are scarcely something more significant than mere puppets in the hands of omnipotent governments or political parties. Their fate is to succumb to the power of the authorities and their struggle to avert the inevitable is typically futile. However, it is fascinating to observe the differences between the main characters and their development within the two novels. The first one is an outspoken symbol of good, the second utterly evil, yet he is to change into a grotesque scapegoat.

Another goal of this work is to take a closer look at other peculiarities of these worlds. The rules and mechanics of corrupted societies are different in both the novels and there are many details to carefully pay attention to. Usually, dystopian novels have a moral, a political and a social aspect. They warn against political threats that typically threaten the democratic way of life and uphold persecution. In the 20th century the uprising of fascism and communism (especially Russian communism) inspired many authors to write their own dystopias. These may have been allegoric like Orwell's *Animal Farm* (1945), very realistic and close to their model or set in a world that is in a very distant future. However, they always point to a real threat by describing its common features. In most 20th century dystopian novels we can find description of real persons and real mechanisms of totalitarian countries. For instance, Napoleon from *Animal*

Farm stands for Stalin, Eurasia in *1984* is what real Soviet Russia might look like in the near future with Thought Police representing KGB and so on. This work presents an analysis of what kind of dystopias we can find in the two mentioned books.

Another goal of this work is to unveil on what basis both dystopian worlds function, which comprises namely of their hierarchical structure, methods of oppression, factors that contributed to and enabled seizure of power in the first place. At the same time, how the political power of leading authorities is being kept and maintained. Although *A Clockwork Orange* is not set in an altogether totalitarian world, it nevertheless contains political struggle for power by using methods that are very close to those of a totalitarian government. The crucial motif of the individual will and individual freedom is substantially important for both the novels.

Both authors were ingenious when it comes to the uses and various purposes of a language. Both created an English language of their own, or to put it more simply, they changed several areas of the English language to achieve different goals. Not only is it intriguing to take a closer look at the changes they made from the point of view of linguistics. The political and social questions that Nadsat and Newspeak arouse are also hardly negligible. It is the importance of speech pecularities in both worlds and what different political and social purposes do Newspeak and Nadsat serve to.

Another key area to analyze is the influence of outer factors that were triggers for both authors to create their dystopias. That means what political and social threats were present during their life and how do the authors reflect them in their novels. Both the novels illuminate very complex worlds and this work compares them from various angles and thus possibly bestows their key motifs and principles.

II. Theoretical part: Background and Inspirations

II.1. Influence and Historical Importance

Big Brother, Winston Smith, Alex and his droogs, *A Clockwork Orange*, *1984*. It is hardly conceivable to what extent these novels influenced life in the second half of the 20th century and quite possibly life of many more generations to follow.

Both the novels represent two different worlds that were (in the time of their first publication) dangerously close to becoming a reality for western countries when they were written. Even for such a conservative country as the United Kingdom. "What you seem to be saying is that *1984* is no more than a comic transcription of the London of the end of the Second World War" (Burgess, *1985* 21). Not only were they a threat to the western world, they were inspired by very real and sinister totalitarian countries from the east. Furthermore, the danger of totalitarianism never ceases to exist as history teaches us. Therefore, both the novels can always be perceived as a warning for further generations. They have had a strong impact on ordinary people, writers and even on the world politics. The latter is especially true for George Orwell's *1984*, which strongly appeals against totalitarianism and it contributed to a mass awareness of evils and potential atrocities of fascism and mainly of Russian communism. "Terms like fascism and communism represent no true polarity, despite the war. They could both, thought Orwell, be contained in some such name as Oligarchic Collectivism" (Burgess, *1985* 36).

However, despite the indisputable good intentions, Orwell's *1984* and *Animal Farm* were vigorously exploited and misinterpreted by the CIA and

4

the US government for the purposes of the Cold War before and particularly after Orwell's untimely death in 1950. "Orwell's last two novels instantly became weapons in the hands of anticommunist defenders of capitalism standing in the opposition against democratic socialism that Orwell endorsed" (Bowker, 406). It is certainly worth considerable attention that even the best intentions towards the society may be easily abused for purposes of propaganda. Perhaps a society that allows something like that to happen is the one that needs dystopian authors and their novels the most.

One of the writers influenced by George Orwell and by his *1984* was Anthony Burgess. His *A Clockwork Orange* is a completely different kind of dystopia but it proves to have achieved similar merits. An extensive number of authors who have deliberately used symbols from this successful novel or somehow have tried to adapt it are overwhelming. It has found its way into souls of young artists and the names Alex, Clockwork Orange, altogether with miscellaneous Nadsatic expressions from the novel have been used in musical adaptations, lyrics of modern bands and in movies. They are also rooted in everyday speech, especially of young people from the punk subculture. However, the book was severely misunderstood by many. Burgess was considered to be an advocate of violence that he enjoys and that he describes in a very joyful way. "I saw that the book might be dangerous because it presented good, or at least harmlessness, as remote and abstract, something for the adult future of my hero, while depicting violence in joyful dithyrambs" (Burgess *Your Time* 61)

Both the novels are deemed as the most important works of mentally matured and well-flourished authors. The enormous amount of copies sold makes the same point very clearly. Both the books show tremendous qualities that even after decades from their first publishing, people still strive to read them. Perhaps it is due to superb depiction of both dystopias,

5

or because of shivering awareness that what you find in the novels might conceal an impending and substantially real danger.

II.2. A Prophecy not Too Far in the Future

Many people have embraced these novels as prophecies. The eloquent title of *1984* (being written in 1948) was a straightforward clue that we are dealing with a prophecy distant some thirty or forty years. Burgess puts the plot of his novel into "not too far in the future". Even though a reader of *A Clockwork Orange* cannot tell the date of the story precisely, he/she is always aware that everything that happens in the novel is not altogether unconceivable and it might very plausibly concern him in the next few years as well. There are no pieces of evidence of immense scientific research or advancement. A reader of *1984* knows the date for sure (even though the protagonist Winston Smith does not), yet, he/she is also aware of its sinister proximity. There are motifs that seem futuristic such as the ever-present screens that constantly spy on every single person. However, the TV had already existed and it had certainly influenced people's life in 1940s. "It was evident then it was going to be a part of everybody's life. Among the ingenuous there was a feeling that the faces that spoke at you were really looking. The TV was intrusive" (Burgess *1985* 23). Burgess very clearly describes the same general apprehension of the TV that had inspired Orwell to use in *1984*.

Perhaps the awareness of this dangerous proximity and plausibility is what makes both dystopias very easily graspable compared to older ones such as *Brave New World* (1932) by Aldous Huxley that takes place in 26th century or *We* (1924) by Yevgeny Zamyatin. "What gave *1984* such power after publishing is the fact that unlike Huxles's *Brave New World* and Zamyatin's *We* it takes place in real post-war London that everybody knew,

6

compared to unclear undefined worlds of the novels mentioned above" (Bowker, 376). However, the novel *We* was highly praised by Orwell in his review for the *Tribune* newspaper and even by Burgess in his essay part of his book *1985*. Motifs from *We* such as constant surveillance, indigestible food and governmentally endorsed anti-sexuality unquestionably inspired Orwell's *1984*. In a note on the text of *1984* by Dr Davison we can find what George Orwell told Gleb Struve in 1944: "I am interested in that kind of book and even keep making notes for one myself that may get written sooner or later" (Orwell V).

The world of *A Clockwork Orange* is virtually almost the same as it was in the real England when the book was published. There are no signs of any significant scientific progress nor does the country seem very different from its model England. There are political tendencies that point out to the threat of impending totalitarianism, yet the country still seems awfully close to the early 1960s England.

II.3. Personal Background

II.3.1 George Orwell

It is vitally important to stress the social and political background and both authors' mental and physical condition under which their books were written and published. George Orwell started writing his novel in 1946 when the world had just witnessed atrocities of Hitler and Stalin and their totalitarian regimes. During World War II, Stalin managed to slightly soften negative reactions and attitudes towards him and his regime in the circumstances of his military efforts against the Nazi regime. However, he never ceased to be a mortal enemy of democracy in the eyes of Orwell who suffered from and witnessed methods of communist oppression when he served in the Spanish Civil War in the late 1930s. It was hardly possible for a man whose friends were tortured and killed by the Russian or pro-Russian communists to approve of such a regime and that he never did. "Orwell made a clear distinction between the Communist ideals of the Russian Revolution and the betrayal of these ideals by the forcible collectivization of agriculture, the Purge Trials, the extermination of opposition partis in Spain and, later on, the Hitler-Stalin Pact" (Meyers 171). Even as a known socialist he borrowed Stalinist regime as a model for his novel *1984*. He always believed in democratic socialism, not the kind of socialism that threatens the democratic way of life. It might have partly been a theoretically victorious Germany that we find in *1984*, yet it much more resembles soviet Russia with the furthest degree of oppression that cannot be escaped nor fought anymore.

George Orwell had another reason to write a novel as gloomy as *1984*. It was his fragile health condition he had struggled with since his childhood and which culminated in the late 1940s in a severe tuberculosis. After the deaths of several closest friends and relatives such as of his father and first wife, he found himself facing approaching death himself, even though he never stopped believing in at least partial recovery. Yet, there is a little doubt that it would not affect his writings. Orwell himself claimed that without the disease, the novel would have turned out better. "I think it is a good idea but the execution would have been better if I had not written it under the influence of TB" (Crick, 546).

II.3.2 Anthony Burgess

Anthony Burgess had to deal with a severe diagnosis as well. "In 1959, he was invalided home from Malaya and his work with the colonial civil

8

service, with a suspected brain tumour. Given a year to live, this man's remarkable resourcefulness led him to write five novels in that year, so as to leave his wife some posthumous income" (Dix 4). After the diagnosis he was given a year to live. *A Clockwork Orange* was written in 1962. That means that Burgess was already two years overdue when the novel was published. It is this vision of the grim reaper lurking in the shadows nearby that greatly influenced both authors when they wrote their crucial novels. Before, in 1944, four soldiers had assaulted Burgess' pregnant wife and she had lost her baby as a result of the attack. This ominous event of their life inspired Burgess to create Alex and his gang who find pleasure in similar abominable acts.

Unlike Orwell, Burgess had an opportunity to serve in the World War II as an educational officer. He was deeply moved by the atrocities of the war. After Orwell's death, Burgess lived in an atmosphere of the Cold War and the atomic war threat when the world as we know it could end in any second. Around the year 1960, many British citizens shared an opinion that groups of young hooligans acting extra-violently are ill and as such, they should be medically treated. "It was the sense of this division between well us and sick them that led me to write, in 1960, a short novel *A Clockwork Orange*" (Burgess, *1985* 91). Even though *A Clockwork Orange* is not situated in a completely totalitarian regime, it is quite natural that totalitarian regimes that flourished and declined during his life enhanced his decision to write a dystopia. His vision is more focused on an invividual product of corrupted values than on corrupted society and its mechanisms as a whole, as in *1984*. Individual freedom is the key motif in his novel.

II.4. Symbolism:

"This is the London of war-time or just after. It's certainly is not a London of prophetic vision" (Burgess, *1985* 25).

1984 is a year of thorough oppression and ultimate suppression of individual freedom. The title was probably introduced by a simple extraposition of the last two digits of the year 1948 when the novel was finished. London in *1984* is very similar to London in 1948 with many autobiographical motifs from Orwell's life: "All things that haunted him such as inquisition, experience of terror in Barcelona, propagandistic machinations both in the ministry of information and in the BBC, being the object of censorship, desperate state of London during the war and mysteries of urban junk-shops, it all was there. Newspeak was motivated by artificial languages such as Esperanto and Basic English, first intended to simplify communication, yet they gave power to hands of those who would manipulate thinking by restricting it" (Bowker 373). Burgess summarizes Orwell's London in his essay part of *1985*: "Well, the Ministry of Truth may certainly be accepted as the Broadcasting House where Orwell worked during war. Headquarters of the BBC."..."Room 101, in the basement of the Broadcasting House, was where Orwell used to broadcast propaganda to India" (Burgess, *1985* 25). Victory Mansions resemble the ruined 19th century houses in London; the gloomy canteen in Ministry of Truth is the canteen in which Orwell dined during his work for the BBC. Victory cigarettes represent those repulsive cigarettes that were given to soldiers during World War II. Elsewhere Burgess reminiscences about the Hate School he was sent to while serving in the army. Methods used in the School resemble Hate Week in *1984* a great deal. "We were taught Hatred of the Enemy" (Burgess, *1985* 22). There are other easily traceable allusions to the real world that contribute to the overall atmosphere of *1984*. In the words of Goldstein and in his professional rise and decline we can distinguish Trotsky, a great idol of Orwell's, who was also demonised by the communist party that he had earlier helped to create. Slogans of the Party can be just as easily read as the omnipresent fascist and communist slogans used for the purposes of propaganda before and during World War II.

The title of *A Clockwork Orange* may have several interpretations; the ones that Anthony Burgess suggests himself in *1985* could understandably make those most close to the reality. Burgess once heard and then had always kept in his mind a popular cockney saying that goes 'queer as a clockwork orange'. He knew that he would use it for a title of a novel once. "When I began to write the book, I saw that this title would be appropriate for a story about the application of Pavlovian, or mechanical, laws to an organism which, like a fruit, was capable of colour and sweetness" (Burgess, *1985* 92). A clockwork orange is what becomes of Alex. He ceases to be a human being when his ability to choose to do whatever he wants is suppressed. By usage of science and biological incentives he turns into a mechanical being that responds to predetermined triggers out of scope of his own mental powers.

While Orwell may partly identify himself with the protagonist Winston Smith, Burgess certainly does not. Alex and his gang represent the gang that had assaulted Burgess' wife in 1944. Burgess may share some of his opinions through the democratic activist F. Alexander, the fictional author of *A Clockwork Orange* in the novel itself. He is the outspoken voice against totalitarianism and Ludovico's Technique.

Symbolism and subtle references to the real world are used in both the novels, but definitely much more frequently in *1984*. That is why *1984* feels far more pessimistic than *A Clockwork Orange*. Naturally, this effect

11

is caused by other factors as well but frequent symbolism plays one of the key roles in the story of *1984*. Numerous allusions to the real world that we can discover in the novel help to illuminate this unique world and it significantly contributes to the novel's grim and utterly depressive atmosphere. Without all the details that were familiar to a citizen of London in 1948, the novel would hardly achieve such a great success and it would hardly convey such a powerful message.

II.5. Origins of Totalitarian Themes

The rise of 20th century totalitarian authorities greatly inspired both the authors. In both the novels we can distinguish numerous oppressive methods that were inspired by these regimes. Developments in science and general technical progress enabled an enhanced control and surveillance of an individual and at the same time it contributed to the invention or improvement of numerous techniques of oppresion. In *1984* and *A Clockwork Orange* we can find suppresion of the individual freedom, constant surveillance, torture, propaganda, manipulation of a language. The government is deliberately carrying all of the mentioned out in order to retain political power of the ruling class. Although the worlds we read about in both novels are fictional, all totalitarian countries have used all these techniques. Even though the fascist regimes cannot be neglected, the strongest inspiration for these techniques may have been drawn from the ideology of soviet Russia.

II.5.1 Methods and Reasons

In every totalitarian state, there is a ruling minority that needs to retain political power. The power is maintained by a cunning and structured oppresion that eliminates any act of individualism. The government uses both terror and surveillance. "Surveillance means that the population is watched; terror means that its members are subject on an unpredictable but large-scale basis to arrest, execution, and other forms of state violence" (Fitzpatrick 190). The totalitarian police are chiefly occupied with political enemies and they are the most important segment of the state's executive power. When Orwell was writing about the Thought Police, the crucial enforcer of the Party's doctrines, he could have been just as easily writing about the KGB or Gestapo. Their key purpose is to track and eliminate enemies of the government. "Revolutions are usually the work of disgruntled intellectuals with the gift of the gab" (Burgess *1985* 37). These independently thinking individuals are the biggest threat to these regimes and therefore they are vigorously purged; imprisoned, tortured and in most occasions murdered. The ambitious members of the ruling minority also pose a certain degree of threat as they may become prone to organizing a putsch.

When potential enemies are being taken care of, the totalitarian government simultaneously needs to keep the masses obedient. Usually, the government employs elaborate methods of propaganda and lies. Anything that is deemed ideologically dangerous gets destroyed or censored. The history is constantly being rewritten so that it complies with the current government's goals and achievements (even though that might be completely made up). "According to the doctrine of partiinost', history was simply a weapon in the class struggle. There was no such thing as objectivity, all science being merely class science, so the scientist could not fail to take sides" (Daniels 233). Thus, any potential revolutionary finds it difficult to draw inspiration from his predecessors because there is virtually no way to obtain any information about them, or, at least, that is what the government strives for. Furthermore, the cenzorship also functions as a

13

filter of another kind of information. A citizen may by no means find out that he could find a better life for himself elsewhere, in a different country.

While these methods are utterly oppresive, there is also the necessity to induce fanatical love for the government and fanatical hatred towards the enemy. These very adjacent feelings help the government to control the masses because they can be easily enthused when proper methods are being used. This love is achieved by the creation of a cult and it can be either the Stalin cult or the admiration of Big Brother. In soviet Russia, every political success was attributed to Stalin and this glory enabled him to be loved by wide masses of people who were completely unaware of the fact that most of it was lies. "Stalin's public image in the 1930s, like the Tsars' before him, was that of a quasi-sacred leader, font of justice and mercy, and benevolent protector of the weak; he was often photographed smiling paternally on shy peasant women and children" (Fitzpatrick 24).

Hatred is evoked in a very simple way. The portraits of the enemy can be seen virtually everywhere and by usage of propaganda the enemy is portrayed in a way that practically compels the citizen to feel the hatred. In contrast, the leader of the government is given characteristics of their greatest guardian. Furthermore, any negative impacts on the citizens that may have been caused by the government (as it might have been in most cases) are unquestionably attributed to the enemy. The government may always blame the enemy for any food scarcity, famine or war. Every piece of evidence of the contrary gets destroyed and witnesses murdered or sent to a work camp.

II.5.2 The Language

In both the novels, there is a large amount of space dedicated to the language. The totalitarian government often manipulates citizens by transforming the language. As the language is the tool to express thoughts, one can easily estimate what the reason for that is. Thinking cannot be fully controlled and, as it is known, totalitarian government endeavours to control every single aspect of a human life. However, it fails to completely penetrate a person's individual mental processes. Yet, the government is capable of controlling a language to a certain degree. The language is taught in schools and it is also learnt from books. The government thus eliminates books with words that are considered inappropriate or even dangerous. At the same time, the language gets further transformed by several methods.

Some words are usually presented in a very negative context in order to imbue the hatred. The word *enemy* was usually given the connotation - the enemy of the class or enemy of the people. "That notion of "class enemies" implied that there were certain fixed categories of persons in Soviet society who were liable to be victims of terror: kulaks, priests, disfranchised "former people" from the old privileged classes, and the like" (Fitzpatrick 191). Words such as war, fight or punishment are typically bound in connection with the enemies of the state. This coexistence is very effective as the citizens always hear of war as a war against imperialism; the punishment is usually a punishment of traitors or enemies of the regime and so on. Therefore their minds begin to perceive them as such. This perpetual ideological influence helps the government to control people's mental processes to a certain degree.

When it comes to dangerous words that could convey any thought connected with democracy or with any hostile regimes for that matter, these

15

connotations are usually dropped. For instance, the word *faith* may begin to be described as "faith in the revolutionary cause" (Wolfe 134). Religious faith simply ceases to exist because that particular connotative meaning had been removed. The words like democracy or freedom are usually described in a very strict and dogmatic fashion so that no complex interpretation is possible anymore. 'The USSR is the most perfect democracy' could be an example of such a rather vague entry.

III. Practical Part – Two Worlds

III.1. Atmosphere of the Cities

London in *1984* is a place of no crime. There are no laws, there is no violence. There is a scarcity of food but nobody dies due to starvation. At least nobody does that we know of. Proles (the proletariat) that constitute 85% of the society have their beer and lottery, and even pornography produced by the government. There is no unemployment whatsoever and neither are racial prejudices. The Party takes steps to abolish problems connected with families and sex. "No wonder the system is universally accepted" (Burgess, *1985* 47). The independently thinking individuals such as Winston Smith represent rotten apples of otherwise perfectly working society and therefore it is a noble cause and responsibility of the Party to cure him from his heresy.

Winston Smith lives in one of the Victory Mansions. It is a bleak, stinky place, where nothing seems to work properly except for the telescreen which is always on and it may be always watching ordinary citizens. "The hall smelt of boiled cabbage and old rag mats" (Orwell 3). The food, beverages, gin and cigarettes all taste horribly. There is a perpetual war so nobody can really object to the quality when brave soldiers need the best equipment to defend the country. The streets and Winston's neighbourhood are safe and nobody needs to worry about being mugged. Usage of sensual images in order to depict a depressive atmosphere was always Orwell's strong point, especially when it comes to the usage of odours. Wherever Winston goes, he first notices the smells. His house smells of boiled cabbage, Victory Gin has a sickly, oily smell, the Parsons' flat smells of sweat, the canteen in the Ministry of Truth is connected with a metallic scent and of course, there is the smell of Victory Gin. When Winston wanders to the pub in the prole zone, he is immediately repulsed by the smell of urine. It seems that everything that is so unpleasant about *1984* also smells terribly. The only remotely pleasant place is Mr Charrington's junk-shop. "The proprietor had just lighted a hanging oil lamp which gave off an unclean but friendly smell" (Orwell 97). The pleasant smell remark is not just a random commentary. It shows that Winston has arrived in an oasis. A place connected with the past, with hardly imaginable times before the Revolution. Not losing a moment he is determined to rent the room in here right away, to have a chance to escape that gloomy and despicable world. Later, when Winston leaves London for a rendezvous with Julia, he is dazzled by the beauty of the country and by the fresh air. Orwell again reminisces of the good old times here. The country represents innocence and recklessness, the last resort of good in this modern society. However, the short moment there is bound to end just like a dream or illusion, because in fact, everything seemingly nice in *1984* is merely an illusion that shatters as soon as the Party wishes.

Alex in *A Clockwork Orange* lives in a very different city, although it is quite conceivable that Burgess also wrote about London, even though the name of the city is never mentioned. Nonetheless, it makes no big difference as the reader is always aware of the fact that the story is situated in a slightly modified England. In *A Clockwork Orange*, there is a very little space dedicated to the description of the nameless city. Now and then the reader comes across several names of streets and squares, but the atmosphere of the city is much more drawn by what is going on in the streets. A house where Alex lives shows some resemblance to Winston's. The elevator never works, halls are dirty and people who live there such as Alex's parents have dull and important jobs.

III.2. The Society

The division of society in Oceania in *1984* is very simple. Proles are inferior people with no rights, assigned to inferior and mostly manual tasks. The rest of the society is divided into the Inner and the Outer Party. Winston Smith is a member of the less privileged Outer Party and he works in one of the Ministries just like any other member of the Outer Party. In the fictional book *The Theory and Practise of Oligarchical Collectivism* by Emmanuel Goldstein (created by the Party itself), the stratas of the society are described as follows:"Big Brother is the guise in which the Party chooses to exhibit itself to the world. His function is to act as a focusing point for love, fear and reverence, than towards an organisation. Below Big Brother comes the Inner Party, its numbers limited to six millions, or somethin less than two per cent of the population of Oceania. Below the Inner Party comes the Outer Party, which, if the Inner Party is described as the brain of the State, may be justly likened to the hands. Below that com the dumb masses whom we habitually refer to as 'the proles'." (Orwell 217).

As to proles, their life is not very much different from what it could have been in 19th century in the times of early industrialization, or in the first half of the 20th century. They might keep complaining but they will never revolt due to their restricted intelligence and due to the fact that their simple needs are always met. The Party makes sure that they are. Other areas of their life are similar to what they have usually been throughout the history of the working class. And lastly, The Inner Party represents the oligarchic group of the privileged who rule the country.

The city where Alex lives is a one that shares a distant resemblance with Orwell's London. Although the laws are not altogether abolished in *A Clockwork Orange* as they are in *1984,* it seems that they get very mildly enforced, especially in the first part of the novel where an old man complains: "It's a stinking world because it lets the young get on to the old like you done, and there's no law nor order no more" (Burgess, *Clockwork* 15). Youngsters like Alex are able to drink milk with drugs because there is no law forbidding it. They can fight during nights and cause riots and there seems to be nobody stopping them. "The bourgeois middle class in the novel have become so quiet and so passive, that the young who have succeeded them have chosen evil as their way of life, as an assertion of the will" (Dix 14).

On the other hand, street violence is only the case of *A Clockwork Orange*, not *1984*. In his essay part of *1985* Burgess explains why: "A strong centralized State, with powerful techniques of terrorization, can keep the streets free of muggers and killers" (Burgesss *1985* 93). This idea suggests that strong and decisive actions towards criminals go hand in hand with totalitarian regimes and such actions are proposed and advocated by the government at the end of *A Clockwork Orange* as the government apparently takes necessary steps in order to establish totalitarianism.

In the first part of the novel Alex eventually has to take responsibility for his felonies. Yet before that happens, it seems that he encounters no problems when he lies in order to skip school or when he invents a fictional job to explain what he does during nights. That, of course, is the case until he is betrayed by his friends and then he finally gets captured by the police. Nevertheless, the city where Alex lives is a paradise for the likes of him, and at the same time, it is a hell on earth for the elderly and law-abiding citizens, just like Alex's parents. "But we don't go out much now. We daren't go out much, the streets being what they are. Young hooligans and so on" (Burgess, *Clockwork* 41). In *1984*, there is no real danger of being assaulted on the streets. Young and old people are free to wander in the streets; they just must not act suspiciously because they are aware that they might be watched at any time. Majority of people, however, do not have to worry about that since they act in accord with the Party's demands. When Winston Smith is wandering in a street in the proles' part of the city, he is thinking to himself: "The blue overalls of the Party could not be a common sight in a street like this. Indeed, it was unwise to be seen in such place, unless you had definite business there" (Orwell, 86). Winston fears that his presence there is suspicious since he has no regular business being there and therefore, he must be considered guilty of a thoughtcrime because the Party controls all regular activities and thoughts of a Party member.

The atmosphere that any act of individualism, being alone or doing something extraordinary can be considered a thoughtcrime that usually results in vaporization is a common state of things in the London of *1984*. Apprehension of being watched during your whole life is a natural feeling for a citizen of Ocenia. Constant fear that you might not return home safe and sound is the atmosphere of the city in *A Clockwork Orange*. At the beginning of the novel there is the brutality of young hooligans, in the end the police brutality from the hands of the same hooligans, now having been recruited by the police.

III.3. Totalitarian Methods

III.3.1 Methods of the Party

The chief aim of the Party is to eradicate individualism. The Party seeks power for its own sake; it does not consider it means to achieve wealth or happiness. It just wants to remain the ruling power for whole eternity. O'Brien tells Winston: "Alone-free-the human being is always defeated. It must be so, because every human being is doomed to die, which is the greatest of all failures. But if he can make complete, utter submission, if he

21

can escape from his identity, if he can merge himself in the Party so that he is the Party, then he is all-powerful and immortal" (Orwell 277). Everything that the Party claims have accomplished is the eternal and indisputable truth. The only illusionary threats to the Party are people like Winston Smith, i.e. independetly thinking individuals who might have dim recollection of the concept of democratic states. However, the era of these people is merely transitional. In the future, past is going to be altered to comply with the needs of the Party, heretics will be vaporised and forgotten and finally, nobody will be able to even think heretically, when Newspeak reaches its perfect form.

Winston Smith hopes that if there is a hope, it lies within the proles, but deep down, he is aware of the fact that this fantasy will never come true and that the Party is in fact eternal. The proles are too dumb to even conceive any idea as tremendous as a revolution. Even if some of them were, there is always a simple solution. "Proletarians, in practise, are not allowed to graduate into the Party. The most gifted among them, who might possible become nuclei of discontent, are simply marked down by the Thought Police and eliminated" (Orwell 218). Therefore the maximum zeal a prole is capable of is to argue about numbers of lottery.

The propaganda of the Party is very simple. It is concerned with demonization of the enemy, i.e. Eurasia or Eastasia and of course their arch-enemy Emmanuel Goldstein. The Party organises events that focus on expression of joint hatred that binds the community together. Everywhere the slogans urging to hate almost everything can be found, except for the Party of course. The Party also informs citizens about the war which is perpetual for apparent reasons. The warfare destroys wealth and that effectively maintains very low standards of living. The reason for that is to easily achieve obedience. When there is a scarcity of everything and at the same time there is the war against commonly hated enemy, the scarcity becomes endurable. Without the war, there would be no excuse for these low standards. The war joins people and encourages their nationalism. With low life standards there is no comfort which during peace time produces idle intellectuals – the chief enemies of the Party.

The Party is constantly changing records and the history. In doing so it achieves the simple goal that nobody can doubt their omnipotence and power. Yet, there are still people who have not yet succumbed to the propaganda and lies of the Party. The Party is aware that it should not condemn and execute these heretics from their own lines. Christianity, fascism and communism taught the Party that. Executing ardent heretics only inspires others. But The Party does not want martyrs. That is why before executing them, the Party actually cures all heretics by means of interrogation and torture. That is what any other imperfect totalitarian state in the past failed to accomplish and that is why they all eventually declined. Ironically, the known enemies of the Party such as Goldstein are eternal and they will never perish, because the Party needs them. But the enemies from within the Party will never be heard of.

The obedience is contrived by hatred but also by ever-present slogans and absolute obedience of Big Brother and the Party. At every corner, citizens are being reminded that Big Brother is watching them and that they should love him. Dumb obedience is not enough though. The Party is unmistakable and it takes care after everyone. Everyone knows that anyone can make it to the leadership, to the Inner Party. "In principle, membership of these three groups is not hereditary. The child of Inner Party parents is in theory not born into the Inner Party. Admission to either branch of the Party is by examination taken at the age of sixteen. Nor is there any racial discrimination, or any marked domination of one province by another. Jews, Negroes, South Americans of pure Indian blood are to be found in the highest ranks of the Party" (Orwell 217). Children are integrated in various organisations are so are their parents. And most of them truly love taking part in these organisations. They love gathering together as they can hate the enemy together. Together they spit on Emmanuel Goldstein during Two Minute Hate, together they adore Big Brother. Thought Police with their torture are perceived as saints because they cure people from crimethink, just like doctors cure cancer. Winston's simple neighbour Parsons tells Winston about his involuntary act of crimethink that he committed in the cell in Ministry of Love: "Between you and me man, I'm glad they got me before it went any further. Do you know what I'm going to say to them when I go up before the tribunal? 'Thank you' I'm going to say, 'thank you for saving me before it was too late' "(Orwell 245). He is going to be tortured and vaporised but he shows them love for it. That is what the Party wants to achieve.

III.3.2 People Turned into Clockwork Oranges

In *A Clockwork Orange*, there is a very little space dedicated to the description of the country and the mechanics that rule it. Still, throughout the book, a reader still gets an image that the country is on the verge of an impending turning point. It is suggested that several changes are to be made and quite plausibly towards totalitarianism. The Minister of the Interior who is visiting the jail where Alex is imprisoned suggests a significant effort towards totalitarianism: "Soon we may be needing all our prison space for political offenders" (Burgess, *Clockwork* 73). Burgess nevertheless focuses much more intently on how the governmental powers use propaganda and how they use individuals for these purposes. In his essay part of *1985*, Burgess explains his key motif employed in *A Clockwork Orange*: "I am committed to the freedom of choice, which means that if I cannot choose to do evil nor can I choose to do good. It is

24

better to have streets infested with murderous hoodlums than to deny individual freedom of choice" (Burgess, *1985* 93).

The intentions of the propaganda are invariably different from those in *1984* as the country is in a stage where totality has not yet broken out. The State and anti-governmental reformists lead by the writer F. Alexander use criminals for the sole intention to influence the upcoming General Election. Ludovico's Technique of curing criminals is vigorously praised by the government as a remedy on all crime. At the same time, it is passionately opposed by voices of a common sense represented by the writer and a prison chaplain who says: "The question is whether such a technique can really make a man good. Goodness comes from within, 6655321. Goodness is something chosen. When a man cannot choose he ceases to be a man" (Burgess, *A Clockwork Orange* 67). The anti-governmental reformist writer F. Alexander expresses his endeavours and then his fears when he tells Alex as follows: "You can be a very potent weapon, you see, in ensuring that this present evil and wicked Government is not returned in the forthcoming election. The Government's big boast, you see, is the way it has dealt with crime these last months."....." Recruiting brutal young roughs for the police. Proposing debilitating and will-sapping techniques of conditioning."..."We've seen it all before," he said," in other countries. The thin end of the wedge. Before we know where we are we shall have the full apparatus of totalitarianism" (Burgess, *Clockwork* 125).

The State is using Alex to justify their actions towards reducing criminality. But in fact they use totalitarian methods when they take away his individual freedom to choose. In the future, they might even control everyone by using same means of treatment as they used on Alex and thus effectively reducing a human being to mere a puppet in the hands of the government. Anyone who would oppose would be taken care of by the brutal and effective police. Yet, at the same time the reformists are trying to kill Alex in an effort to use him against the government. Even though they might find comfort in that whatever they did, they did in the name of higher good, this method would easily pass as a totalitarian one as well. It is the recurring motif of suppressing an individual freedom in favour of the whole.

III.4. Dystopias Side by Side

There is a strong link to *1984* where Winston also cannot really choose. His only choice is to love Big Brother, nothing else. During one of the interrogations, O'Brien tells him: "Whatever the Party holds to be truth is truth. It is impossible to see reality except by looking through the eyes of the Party" (Orwell 261). Presently, governments both in *1984* and in *A Clockwork Orange* can tell what is good and what is evil. Burgess himself considered this choice the fundamental point of his book.

When we try to compare both the novels and principals of their governmental powers and propaganda, there are naturally many differences. Orwell pays great attention to the functioning of the oligarchic collectivism while Burgess scarcely mentions anything remotely close to such deep political analysis. However, there is a common ground. In both the novels, it is openly suggested that an individual is expendable and unimportant. What matters is the Party and the State as a whole. Individuals such as Alex or Emmanuel Goldstein are made famous because they can be excellently used for purposes of propaganda. Intellectual individuals like Winston Smith or the writer F. Alexander are rotten apples that are taken care of in silence. The aim of the government is to turn them into oblivion as their heresy is dangerous and they have to be silenced. The suppression of revolt altogether with its prevention is a key factor for the preservation of any totalitarian regime.

The means of achieving control are similar in both the novels as well. In both, a sophisticated method of terror is invented in order to enforce obedience. In *A Clockwork Orange,* the State is just in the beginning of using these methods as Alex is the first human to be a subject for Ludovico's Technique. However, this technique is as inhumane, cunning and efficient as those in *1984.* Absolute control of history, permanent oligarchic reign, and elimination of opposition, everything that works in *1984* can be just as easily contrived by thorough usage and further-development Ludovico's Technique. When the government finds means to control a human mind, it can do whatever it wishes.

III.5. Winston Smith and Alex and their Development throughout the Novel

III.5.1 Hero vs. Antihero

Winston Smith may be the voice of George Orwell. Or at least he is a part of him. He is intelligent yet he lives in a misery (much like George Orwell's life). Physically he is not in a very good shape but his is job is quite mentally challenging. By usage of doublethink (method of absorbing two contradictory statements and accepting both as valid at the same time) he corrects history in accordance with demands of the Party. But Winston Smith sinned. He sinned in the eyes of the almighty Party. Even though his memory is hazed, he somehow feels that what the Party does is not right. He feels that before the Revolution, a human race must have been better off. He finds an inception that whatever the Party represents should be fought and destroyed. However, his thoughts are still very dim and confused until he reads the book *The Theory and Practice of Oligarchical*

Collectivism wrote by an arch-enemy of the Party Emmanuel Goldstein. Later, he is to find out it was written by the Party itself.

Alex also represents a rotten apple of the society. Although there are presumably many more likes of Alex in *A Clockwork Orange* than many other Winstons Smiths in *1984*. As a character, Alex is a true anti-hero. He is vile, hypocritical and extremely aggressive. He lives on the edge of the society. He uses drugs, beats up innocent people, and commits a rape and eventually even a murder. Yet, quite surprisingly, a reader is almost imperceptibly pushed throughout the novel into sympathizing with him in a way and later even feeling sorry for him.

Unlike Winston Smith he is in the peak of his physical strength but he is very intelligent just like Winston. He is dangerous to fellow citizens while Winston threatens the principals of the State. When Winston Smith conceives the first thought of heresy, he already knows he is dead. His vital struggle is to live undetected as long as it is possible. That is even truer after he involves in a rather physical relationship with Julia – a deliberate act of revolt. Such relationships are obviously strongly forbidden. Little does he know that he had been already detected a long time ago. After his capture by the Thought Police, there is a little hope. In the beginning he is determined to remain unchanged. He knows that he is in right in his fight and that he stands on the side of the good, on the side of the past. In spite of that, after a lengthy captivity consisting of torture and interrogations he is eventually broken and cured. Cured from the point of view of the Party. He gets changed from a rebel into a worshipper of Big Brother. Thus the Party effectively completed its reign of terror by defeating the last stand of humanity.

Alex gets captured as well. He is convicted and the first thing he does in prison is killing again. After two years in a prison his character does not change a bit. He gets even more hypocritical as he pretends to have become a good Christian and he does not stop dreaming of acts of his favourite ultra-violence. When he is chosen to undergo Ludovico's Technique, as it is called, he is effectively cured very much like Winston Smith. He also suffers during the harsh procedure and eventually he is turned into a human-being unable to choose between good and evil. Furthermore, the doctors unintentionally manage to associate his repulsion towards violence and evil with beautiful Beethoven's symphonies. "The unintended destruction of Alex's capacity for enjoying music symbolizes the State's imperfect understanding (or volitional ignorance) of the whole nature of man, and of the consequences of its own decisions. We may not be able to trust a man – meaning ourselves – very far, but we must trust the State far less" (Burgess, *1985* 93).

The individual freedom in *1984* is very much restricted to freedom to love Big Brother and the Party and at the same time to hate enemies of the Party. This applies mainly for the members of the Party. The individual freedom in *A Clockwork Orange* can be easily suppressed by the government by Ludovico's Technique that can effectively make a person do whatever the government wants him to do and not to do.

III.5.2 The Beginning of the End.

Both protagonists eventually wind up as walking mindless bodies. Alex is forced to attempt to commit a suicide. Winston who has been reduced to his shadow is dully awaiting a bullet in the back of the head.

Winston Smith represents very sparse minority that is harmful to the Party. Of course the Party knows very well how to handle the likes of his; they cannot nonetheless afford to underesetimate these dangers. He also symbolises the last hope of democracy that is slowly deteriorating and

29

eventually bound to extinct. He finds himself in a point of transition where the totalitarian regime is very close to achieve perfection. When Winston Smith is cured, his memories and ideals that he represented finally perish. Thus, the Party becomes immortal and indestructible. George Orwell originally considered the title of the novel *The Last Man in Europe* and with the death of Winston Smith it seems that with the last man of the old era died, he is now being replaced by a completely new type of a human.

Alex demonstrates a turning point as well. As he is the first person turned into a puppet completely in the hands of the government, he may trigger an era of utter totalitarianism where the State can alter the minds of citizens in any way it wishes to. Thus creating a totalitarian regime with no real danger of revolution and with a stable dominion, quite possibly also oligarchic. It seems that the process of treatment of the protagonists and its eventual success triggers very dark repercussions for both the worlds.

Both the protagonists are very naive and they do not understand the complicated world that they live in. They find themselves in the epicentre of deep political interests and it happens almost unintentionally (that is especially true for Alex). Winston Smith has a deep feeling that what is happening in the society is wrong; his view is nevertheless very dim and naive. Alex has no idea whatsoever why both State and the reformists try to use him and, inevitably, he is bound to end up a victim.

III.5.3 Betrayal and How Protagonists are Being Used.

The atmosphere of betrayal keeps recurring throughout both the novels and it has significant impact on both protagonists. Winston Smith gets betrayed by Julia, Julia by Winston, Winston by O'Brien, Winston by Mr Charrington. In *A Clockwork Orange*, Alex first gets betrayed by his gang,

30

later by his parents (or at least in his eyes), eventually by reformists and to a certain degree, by the government itself as well.

1984 is a world where you can never feel safe. It is a world where children are taught to tell on their parents and they feel no remorse when they condemn them to death. Smith's neighbours the Parsons have children who are utterly brainwashed by the propaganda of the Party, as they are members of Spies created by the Party to teach children to spy on everyone. The kids yell on Winston when they mark them as a potential a traitor and in the third part of the book, Winston finds out that the daughter of Mr. Parsons denounced her own father for speaking out thoughtcrimes in his dreams.

When Winston starts relationship with Julia, he can never be sure that she will not turn him in eventually. Then, O'Brien represents a last hope that the Party could be destroyed. But when Winston realises he was deceived his hopes vanish. Winston is determined never to subdue to the torture, yet eventually when he is brought into contact with his mortal enemy, he betrays Julia, his only love. Just like Julia betrays him. He is eager to say anything to save himself, even to pass his punishment on her. Orwell dreadfully shows that a human being can be made to say and do anything that the tormenter wishes. "There are occasions when a human being will stand out against pain, even to the point of death. But for everyone there is something unendurable – something that cannot be contemplated. Courage and cowardice are not involved. If you are falling from a height it is not cowardly to clutch at a rope. If you have come up from deep water it is not cowardly to fill your lungs with air. It is merely an instinct which cannot be disobeyed. It is the same with the rats. For you, they are unendurable. They are a form of pressure that you cannot withstand, even if you wished to. You will do what is required of you" (Orwell 298).

It is dreadfully close to what Alex is made into by what is also called a curing process with certain euphemism. It nevertheless much more resembles the torture from *1984*. When he is betrayed by his gang, he gets imprisoned. A reader, however, is quite aware that the treachery of his gang was inspired by Alex himself and by his questionable leadership of the gang. Therefore is does not provoke the conscience of a reader. Not even after his cellmates all stick together in their witness that Alex is the one responsible for the death of a newly coming cellmate. The consequences of betrayals that are to follow are much more severe. When Alex is offered to undergo the Ludovico's Technique, he is completely unaware what is going to become of him. His sole intention is to circumvent the system and to achieve his release as soon as possible. He laughs at them inside when he is told he will have no evil intentions in two weeks' time.

Alex is eventually cured and he is in a way betrayed by the government as he could not have predicted what they would turn him into. It is plausible that had he known, he would not have undergone the procedure. After his final release, he soon realizes what became of him. When he finds himself in the hands of F. Alexander, he is assured he is going to be well taken care of (again). He truly believes the writer yet he gets betrayed again. And for what other purposes than propaganda. F. Alexander and his associates want him to commit suicide in order to discourage voters from supporting the government. When they fail, Alex does not get betrayed anymore, but the exploitation seems to be never-ending. As in every good totalitarian state, F. Alexander gets removed (quite possibly vaporized) and Alex is used by the government again, this time to show how dangerous reformists are and all the government thinks of is to care about the good of citizens and of poor old Alex.

Both protagonists get betrayed over and over again while both authors prove a point. They illuminate worlds where treachery is a method to ensure that the governing powers remain in their seats. It is impossible to maintain a totalitarian regime without deliberate efforts to betray anyone whenever it is necessary. This vital principle is embodied in every totalitarian regime and that may be the reason why Orwell and Burgess implemented it so frequently into their novels. The only important thing is to have the power, everything is allowed when it means that the Party or the government retains the power. The end justifies the means.

The oligarchs that rule these countries are also aware that what they do cannot be open to the public. They do not want martyrs or any records of them. Betrayal is an effective weapon in hands of the government, but it must by all means remain undiscovered by common people.

III.6. Newspeak and Nadsat

III.6.1 Brief Analyssis

Newspeak and Nadsat serve to very different purposes. At the same time, they create inherent part of both books and they illuminate an atmosphere that makes both the novels truly memorable for. Some of the words invented found their way into everyday speech such as the Big Brother – now a symbol for governmental oppression and surveillance. And many young people frequently use familiar terms like *tolchock* or *moloko*.

From the linguistic point of view, it is fascinating to take a closer look on both. Certainly there is the new vocabulary. Orwell's Newspeak removed all irregularities from verb endings and also in plurals. Negation became a powerful means of further reduction of the vocabulary. "Given, for instance, the word *good*, there was no need for such a word as *bad*, since the required meaning was qually well-indeed, better-expressed by *ungood*" (Orwell 315). New words are usually created by affixation or blending and their meaning can be very easily guessed, although the meaning conveyed is somewhat broader compared to Oldspeak (English of the first half of the 20th century). Blending was a common method in the beginning of the 20th century. "It had been noticed that the tendency to use abbreviations of this kind was most marked in totalitarian countries and totalitarian organisation. Examples were such words as *Nazi, Gestapo, Comintern, Inprecor, Agitprop*" (Orwell 320). These were predecessors of words like *thinkpol, Minipax, Ingsoc* and so on. Some of the blends curiously express the opposite meaning. For instance, *Minitrue* standing for Ministry of Truth where Winston works is a departement that falsifies past and constantly revises history as to remove anything potentially harmful to the Party. However, Ministry of Lies is not a very conveniant propagandistic title.

Burgess invented an argot that is used by young people. It absorbs words mainly from Russian and some other minor languages such as gypsy and Malay. Its main word-formation process is borrowing. Most words have same or very close to pronunciation as their models. Their spelling is usually changed in order to be read correctly by an English speaking reader. Some words are even changed completely on a basis of phonetic resemblance. A good example can be the word *horrorshow* that comprises two common English words and it constitutes a new compound word that is close to its Russian model *khorosho* in pronunciation and almost identical in meaning. All the words share morphematic regularities with their English counterparts. That means that the regular ending in plural forms, in verbs in the third person and so on is maintained.

There is a small gap in the story, though, perhaps unintentional. A reader does not know what the source of Nadsat is. Usage of so many words from Russian would suggest some kind of dominion or at least an increased social interaction, nevertheless no clues to prove that are provided. "Nothing is told about the history or whereabouts of this strange futuristic society, but the deductions are there in the language. The society obviously has been subject to both American and Russian intervention if not invasion. The derivative language, spoken by the young, probably indicates the effects of propaganda through subliminal penetration" (Dix 14).

We can distinguish certain resemblance between these two languages from the grammatical point of view. Both Nadsat and Newspeak use adverbs with the *–wise* suffix. While Newspeak use this suffix exclusively for all adverbs, Nadsat use it for some, yet much more frequently than they are used in English.

III.6.2 Other Language Finesses in *A Clockwork Orange*

What is staggering is the eloquence with which Alex often likes to speak. He is capable of a complete transgression of codes as he occasionally switches to a very noble and polite register of language. That usually happens when he is talking with adults or authorities. At the same time, we feel that in doing so he is being ironic and that he amuses himself to talk like that from time to time. He even uses very obsolete words. This seems to be put into contrast with his very low and animal-like behaviour to achieve rather absurd and comic effect. "Never fear. If fear thou hast in thy heart, O brother, pray banish it forthwith" (Burgess, *Clockwork* 20). That is a sentence from Shakespearian world, yet it is used as an introduction to merciless beating and rape. Clearly, Burgess contrives to illuminate very absurd contrast between these two.

Burgess also successfully attempted to use prosody to enrichen his book as well. This is particularly noticable in the description of a skirmish with Alex's foes, Billyboy and his gang. "And, my borthers, it was real satisfaction to me to waltz –left two three, right two three – and carve left cheeky and right cheeky," (Burgess, *Clockwork* 17). It is a brutal fight, yet Alex describes it as something beautiful, as if it was even some kind of art or even a dance. The rhytm of the actual dance waltz is very apparent there. Once again it is very distinguishable that Burgess tries to connect brutal acts with noble descriptions. It is certainly one of the reasons why is Alex's storytelling so intriguing.

III.6.3 Purposes and Effects

The new vocabulary of Newspeak has quite opposite aims than the new vocabulary of Nadsat. While Nadsat invents new words and thus broadens the vocabulary, the purpose of Newspeak is to eliminate as many words as possible and cut the word-stock to the bone. Nadsat functions as means of young people to alienate themselves from the society of adults. It represents a rebellion where everything connected with adults is wrong, even the language they speak. It does not have deep political purpose nor does it change the way young people think or behave. That is very contrary to effects of Newspeak.

Purpose of Newspeak is not alienation, it is integration. Newspeak vigorously eliminates huge amount of words in order to establish a language that is almost free of any thoughts. "The purpose of Newspeak was not only to provide a medium of expression for the world-view and mental habits proper to the devotees of Ingsoc, but to make all other modes of thought impossible. It was intended that when Newspeak had been adopted once and for all and Oldspeak forgotten, a heretical thought – that

36

IV. Conclusion

Both the novels depict two different fictional Englands that share several features with their real counterparts. *A Clockwork Orange* was certainly much closer to the reality when it was written. There was a strong reason to fear that a party with similar proposal as Ludovico's Technique could win an election and then start abusing it. *1984* shows more distant future yet there are many links to the London of 1948 when it was written. Even though the collectivistic regime in *1984* is very elaborate and perhaps evens more oppressive than 20th century totalitarian regimes, there was no way of knowing that the soviet regime would not have reached such perfection in the future. *1984* has always been less likely to become the reality than *A Clockwork Orange*, yet it has always standed for a warning that it is not impossible.

The atmosphere of both the novels is very grim yet the overall atmosphere of *1984* seems grimmer due to the extremity of various methods used by the government. A regular citizen in *A Clockwork Orange* still has a certain degree of dignity and individual freedom even though he lives in a fear he might get assaulted virtually anytime he/she leaves a house. A regular citizen in *1984,* excluding members of the Inner Party, is reduced to a mindless clockwork body only capable of limited feelings and thoughts. One must love the Big Brother, hate the enemy and at the same time he/she must fear the Party. Those are the basic feelings a citizen is restricted to. What is to become of regular citizens in *A Clockwork Orange* after the General Election is not mentioned. Quite plausibly, the Ludovico Technique would become a powerful tool of control of human minds by the government but it is not certain. However, the majority of people are not oppressed as it is usual in totalitarian countries. The ordinary citizens of

1984 are more or less destined to succumb to the power of the Party. With the effective usage of terror and elaborated ways of controlling the minds, it seems that after the likes of Winston Smith will eventually vanish; there is no stopping the Party's eternal reign.

In both the novels we can discover how totalitarian goverments justify their methods by usage of propaganda. Alex is used to show how the government ingeniously eradicates crime. What are the other negative consequences both for Alex and for the society the government does not speak about. Voices against the government are silenced. The same motif is inherent for *1984* as well. Any potentional enemy is eliminated and masses are kept obedient by lies. The enemy is being attributed with everything that is negative for the society and everything positive is attributed to the Party or Big Brother.

Both the protagonists live through similar experiences. In rotten societes they live in they first find little pleasures of life only to be later crushed by the omnipotent governments. They get betrayed and then tortured. Alex's treatment can be hardly perceived as anything different than torture. The tortures and their results illustrate how governments or any other political authorities may achieve almost anything when it comes to the manipulation of an individual when appropriate methods are used. Alex and Winston get eventually "cured" and thus they symbolise that the government is far stronger than an individual.

The comparison of the slang Nadsat in *A Clockwork Orange* and Newspeak shows that both were used to achieve very different goals and they have almost nothing in common. The slang is used to alienate youngsters from the mainstream society and it widens the vocabulary. It suggests a certain degree of influence by Russia on England as the words are mostly of the Russian origin, however, no such pieces of evidences are provided in the novel. Newspeak eliminates as many words as possible and it is being developed for the mainstream society to easily integrate it for the purposes of oligarchic collectivism. It does not have any artistic ambitions, its sole intention and primary goal is to reduce thinking by reducing the vocabulary.

Both the novels are two of the most crucial dystopias of the 20th century. Their warning against totalitarianism has had a significant impact on wide public and the messages they convey prove to be everlasting as they still attract great number of readers even some fifty or sixty years after they were published for the first time. The dystopian motifs in the novels are described in very persuasive way as most of the motifs correspond with developments of actual totalitarian regimes and with actual totalitarian tendencies in the 20th century Europe.

Works Cited

Burgess, Anthony. *1985.* London: Hutchinson, 1978.

Burgess, Anthony. *A Clockwork Orange.* London: Penguin Books, 1972.

Burgess, Anthony. *You've Had Your Time.* New York: Grove Weidenfeld, 1990.

Crick, Bernard. *George Orwell: A Life.* New York: Penguin Books, 1982.

Dix, Carol M. *Anthony Burgess.* London: Longman Group LTD, 1971.

Meyers, Jeffrey. *Orwell.* New York: Norton, 2000.

Orwell, George. *1984.* London: Penguin Book, 1989

Wolfe, Bertram D. *Communist Totalitarianism.* Boston: Beacon Press, 1956.

Druck: KN Digital Printforce GmbH · Schockenriedstraße 37 · 70565 Stuttgart